BRAZIL FADO

Megan Terry

directed and structured by
Jo Ann Schmidman

BROADWAY PLAY PUBLISHING INC
New York
www.broadwayplaypublishing.com
info@broadwayplaypublishing.com

Cover photo by Megan Terry
I S B N: 978-0-88145-648-6
First printing: June 2016
Book design: Marie Donovan
Page make-up: Adobe InDesign
Typeface: Palatino
Printed and bound in the U S A

BRAZIL FADO was first produced as an experimental try-out at the Omaha Magic Theatre, 21–30 January 1977.

A full production with musical score by Marianne de Pury was produced by Santa Fe Theatre Arts Corp, 14–30 June 1978. The cast and creative contributor were:

BARTON .... Jimmy Jess Sternfeld
DANIELLE .... Karen Thibodeau

Ensemble .... Denise Chavez, Allan Macrae,
Laurie Macrae, Michael Robertson,
Rosalie Traina

Director .... Jo Ann Schmidman
Set .... The Ensemble & M Terry

CHARACTERS

In America:
DANIELLE
BARTON, *a married couple*

In Brazil:
NEWSCASTERS
FRED ASTAIRE
GINGER ROGERS
CARMEN MIRANDA
PEASANTS
POLICE
GUERILLAS
OFFICIALS
CORPORATE SPOKESPERSONS
PRISONERS
PORNOGRAPHY SALESPERSON

Those in the Brazilian section transform. Four or more actors may play all the parts.

SETTING

The play's action is set in two places: DANIELLE *and*
BARTON *in an American home; the other characters are
broadcasters in a television station or represent images that
emanate from that station.*

*The setting: the play takes place in two playing areas.
actually two plays are going on at once. The American home
is on a high platform behind and "above" the television
station. (If your theatre's ceiling is high enough you could
have a double-decker stage as we did at the Omaha Magic
Theatre. For the production in Santa Fe, since the ceiling
was only eight feet, we cut down all the furniture in the T
V station, so that the platform playing area for the american
home "appeared" higher to the audience. We also cut off the
audience chairs in ever rising graduations, to give the feeling
of height) but not too high. Be sure that it is physically
comfortable for the audience to look at both playing spaces.
For the American home, all that is needed is a chaise or a
small couch, one rose lamp and a few props, and perhaps
some luscious draperies behind the chaise. For the television
station, two tables to act as desks, under which props may
be stored. use stage side walls to hang the props and musical
instruments. Since actors will be doing intense physical
work, it's a good idea to have a rug or thick ground cloth for
the playing area.*

This play is dedicated to the memory of
Momo & Reggie
& all of those who work for social Justice

(All transform to "Americans" on a visit to Brazil. They snap photos, point, dance an out-of-rhythm Samba.)

NEWSCASTER 3: I want to play like Pelé—

NEWSCASTER 5: Lose myself in Mardi Gras melee—

NEWSCASTER 1: With a hundred million Brazillions!

NEWSCASTER 2: I want to dance the samba
Until I get my fill
In Brazil, Brazil, Brazil, Brazil, Brazil, …Brazil… *(Fade out)*

(They continue harmony as song fades. One actor transforms into a bulldozer clearing jungle land. The others turn backs as song continues to fade, then turn out to watch demolition but cover eyes, mouths or ears. One actor stands with back to audience and rips his shirt up the back. Projection map of Brazil appears and disappears. NEWSCASTER 4 transforms into Carmen Miranda and circles the playing area to tune of Tico Tico.)

(Ethel Smith on organ)

(DANIELLE and BARTON are at home in America. She reclines on a chaise wearing Fredericks of Hollywood nightwear. She plays to a home video camera.)

(The audience is the camera.)

(BARTON exercises stage left.)

DANIELLE: *(To camera and audience)* Hello. I'm the owner of this body—my person. I'm at the point where I'm willing to spend money.

(Their room is a shrine to the Hell's Angels. But instead of S & M items like rubber, leather, chains and whips, the tools BARTON *will use on* DANIELLE *are a bathroom plunger, a plastic plain mister, a hair-wash faucet attachment, a feather duster, a wooden meat tenderizer, a bottle cleaner and a mop head. He does yoga, karate, kung fu and deep breathing exercises. He is deeply involved with his own body.* CARMEN MIRANDA *comes forward again and dances to a short burst of fado music. She continually moistens her lips.* DANIELLE *flirts with audience.)*

CARMEN MIRANDA: We bring you... *(A Flamenco stomp)* ...now... *(Stomp becomes a dance)*

*(*NEWSCASTERS *move to two news desks up stage. All smile at camera and perform torture on themselves.)*

NEWSCASTER 2: *(Twisting her arm behind her back)* Now...

NEWSCASTERS 1 & 4: *(One pulling out her fingernails, the other slapping her face)* Now...

NEWSCASTERS 3 & 5: *(One strangling self, the other smashing head on desk)* Now...

CARMEN MIRANDA: ...The *(Rolling her Rs)* report of...

*(*NEWSCASTERS *3 and 5 are pulled together by a magnetic force. They connect at their third eyes, struggle to resist the force, finally pull selves around to face out, still connected, and say line.)*

NEWSCASTERS 3 & 5: ...the Third Eye Blues.

*(*NEWSCASTERS *3, 4 and 5 transform into guerilla fighters or Brazilian peasants who blink tiny flashlights and search.)*

NEWSCASTERS 1 & 2: *(Behind desks)* Millions of eyes move on the map.

(They too transform into guerillas or peasants—the line is repeated until it becomes a jam.)

(While BARTON *exercises:)*

DANIELLE: It isn't easy to stand up in front of people. It is if you think about it. I don't mean think about it. I mean it's easy in your mind's eye to stand up in front of people if you dream about it.

(The peasants/guerillas pop up from behind the broadcast desks.)

NEWSCASTER 5: Highlights—

NEWSCASTER 1: Lowlights—

NEWSCASTER 2: Revelations—

NEWSCASTERS 3 & 4: *(Turn to camera/audience)* — eyelights on Brazil. *(They repeat the lines building to a jam. From behind the desks they transform back and forth [very fast].)*

(From romantic movie images to sleazy night club images as they jam.)

(While BARTON exercises:)

DANIELLE: In fact, I think if a lot of people would be honest, they would like to stand up and say a few things that are on their mind. I know my grandfather used to talk back to the T V all the time. It would make me mad a lot when he did that, but now that he's gone I find that I'm doing it. I talk back a lot. I didn't notice it so much till when I was at the movies, people started to tell me to shut up, and I talked right back at them, too. Right out loud in a movie house.

(NEWSCASTER with brick in mouth moves slowly on knees side to side between broadcast desks. The other four sit in pairs back to back, one couple on each news desk.)

DANIELLE: It's crazy because I'm grown up. I never did things like that when I was little. I only talked back to the movie screen at the movies when I was really a little kid, before I knew what it was all about. The only thing I yelled at was when they kissed. I wanted them to get on with the show.

(BARTON flings DANIELLE from the chaise and delicately places a clear plastic drop cloth over it to protect it from spills. Two pairs of NEWSCASTERS transform into FRED ASTAIRE and GINGER ROGERS. They spin to the fronts of the desks and dance.)

DANIELLE: *(Crouching in corner of platform)* What I've noticed lately is that I spend a lot of time alone.

(NEWSCASTER with brick in mouth takes it out, jumps on news desk left, transforms into GINGER ROGERS and tap-dances.)

ROGERS: Once your mother was a hostage of Astaire.

DANIELLE: I like to be alone.

ASTAIRE: They danced without a care down the isles of the Caribbean.

(They spin their GINGERS who twirl around in circle-continue through next lines.)

DANIELLE: I think I like to be alone a lot.

ASTAIRE: *(Back to back with Fred Astaire. Cool to audience)* You weren't even a gleam yet and your father wouldn't have you on a bet.

DANIELLE: But I'm very used to myself alone…

(The GINGERS twirl center, connect and do a beautiful dip together.)

(Holding dip, small, soft smile to audience)

ROGERS: But flying down to Rio was one reality.

(DANIELLE seductively approaches BARTON, who turns away from her—she settles onto the chaise.)

DANIELLE: …and I'd like more variety in my life.

(The tap-dancing GINGER *on top of the desk transforms into the* BRIDE OF FRANKENSTEIN. NEWSCASTERS 1 *and 3 transform into police who search her—they shine flashlights in her eyes, search her body to make her talk.* NEWSCASTERS 4 *and 5 move slowly forward and back on knees giving themselves a self -examination with flashlights—actors should work on the feeling of helplessness one feels when being examined.)*

BRIDE OF FRANKENSTEIN: *(Rather rapidly—direct explanation)* My first psychiatrist was from Brazil.

*(*BARTON *throws* DANIELLE *down and arranges her in position on plastic-covered chaise. During her next several lines he demonstrates rubber gloves. When he uses household items on her, he focuses on her buttocks breasts, inner thighs.)*

*(*DANIELLE *flirts with* BARTON *who pays no attention to her:)*

DANIELLE: I noticed that I tend to say things in a different way…

BRIDE OF FRANKENSTEIN: His name was Houruz Vitale Brazil.

(The Brazilian police guards begin to search her body)

DANIELLE: …feel other things, see ideas in a new light when other people are present. Like something I might be dead set against when I'm alone…

BRIDE OF FRANKENSTEIN: He told me I didn't have to push people in front of subway trains.

(One guard shoves flashlight up her ass.)

DANIELLE: I might tend to go along with…

BRIDE OF FRANKENSTEIN: *(Speaks quickly, clawing the air in pain from rectal intrusion)* He told me to stop thinking about Sputnik and the Russian military, technological and scientific advancement which would make the

Americans a second-class power, and focus on what I was avoiding.

(As BARTON *blows up gloves and demands that* DANIELLE *suck the fingers:)*

DANIELLE: …if I'm with one or two other people.

(As police guards pick up long board and hold it on a horizontal plane above her head to symbolize administering of electric shock:)

BRIDE OF FRANKENSTEIN: He said he wouldn't abandon me but he did. He had to return to Brazil for personal reasons.

(Guards place board across her breasts.)

DANIELLE: Sometimes I'd even change my vote…

BRIDE OF FRANKENSTEIN: *(Laugh-cries from the pleasure-pain of the electric shock)* He was very beautiful and gentle and would laugh at me. He thought my love affairs exotic.

(They place the board across her groin.)

DANIELLE: *(Enjoying sucking)* …after talking with people over a few drinks.

*(*BARTON *pulls away from* DANIELLE *and puts on the gloves—she feels deserted.)*

(As they place the board across her forehead:)

BRIDE OF FRANKENSTEIN: Here he was from Brazil telling me that my love affairs were exotic.

(They hold the board above her head)

BRIDE OF FRANKENSTEIN: I might never have gone to see him every week if he hadn't come from Brazil.

DANIELLE: You shouldn't try to run the world all by yourself.

(The BRIDE OF FRANKENSTEIN *and one of the "attendants"
move to opposite upstage corners and transform into police,
one with knife in mouth, the other armed.* NEWSCASTERS
4, 5 *and* 1 *transform into a Brazilian family asleep in
their home. They rest on a wooden stick which they hold
diagonally, resting a head, arm, wrist or torso on it. The
bodies arrange together on the diagonal stick to create a
"sleep image," the two police slowly and silently sneak up on
the sleeping family. One breaks down the door to their home,
the other enters through a window. They grasp the ends of
the diagonal "sleep stick" and vibrate it—this separates the
husband from the wife and child. the police use the stick to
beat the family [symbolically]) across the beck and gut in two
sharp moves. Then they place the stick between the husband
and his family and move it slowly back and forth, pushing
first the wife and child, then the husband, then the wife, and
child, then the husband, when the husband is separated far
enough from his family, he is tortured and the wife forced
to watch. danielle moistens her lips seductively, flirts with
camera/audience. She begins speaking when the family wakes
from the police vibrating the stick. barton demonstrates mop
head as hair, whip and magic fingers, displays the power of
his stroke by whistling it through the air. he may use karate
sounds.)*

DANIELLE: *(As* BARTON *begins whipping her with mop
head, building to a climax)* Lately I've been trying to
break myself of chewing on my lips when I'm alone.

*(*DANIELLE *freezes—a "stop-frame" on video—with image
of "horrible lips",)*

DANIELLE: I'm scared to death I'll do that when I'm
out with someone. *(Freezes in "confidence" image to
camera. Moistens lips)* I caught myself doing that in the
bathroom mirror yesterday. *(Sees frightening image in
mirror, freezes)*

(At this point the Brazilian husband cries out from torture. The wife who's being forced to watch also cries out. the torture continues again in silence. A single, repeated emblematic "torture" move can be used.)

DANIELLE: It's gross.

(BARTON abruptly stops whipping DANIELLE and leaves her before she can reach a climax. Both are very excited, but he, being "master," can stop the activity as he sees fit.)

(The two police leave. one transforms back into NEWSCASTER 3 and appears with NEWSCASTER 4 at upstage left news desk.)

DANIELLE: I hate it and I'm doing all I can to stop.

(The two NEWSCASTERS Are in a hurry to report this news, and on guard for anyone who may be police. It is urgent that they broadcast this news to the people.)

NEWSCASTER 3: We have had eyewitness reports that Brazilian torture police were trained in Washington, DC, in the latest torture methods.

(Thinking [s]he hears someone coming, NEWSCASTER 4 covers NEWSCASTER 3's mouth. They freeze, terrified. NEWSCASTER 4 releaseS NEWSCASTER 3 when the danger has passed.)

NEWSCASTER 3: Some women find it hard to believe that their men had to go to Washington, DC, to learn the art of torture, but it is in the hearsay record of the common folk.

(Thinking [s]he hears something, NEWSCASTER 3 covers NEWSCASTER 4's mouth. They freeze, terrified. NEWSCASTER 3 releases NEWSCASTER 4 when the danger is past.)

NEWSCASTER 2: The folk who've had their relatives taken from them in the night and locked up with electrodes up their asses.

(NEWSCASTERS 2 *and* 5 *transform into terrorists and put paper bags over* NEWSCASTERS 3 *and* 4, *who scream. When* NEWSCASTER 2 *speaks,* NEWSCASTER 5 *keeps* NEWSCASTERS 3 *and* 4 *under close surveillance.*)

(BARTON *demonstrates a rubber shower attachment.*)

NEWSCASTER 2: *(Urgently, as if it were a flash flood or a tornado warning)* Special from the New York Times, Sunday, January 5th, 1975 Brazil lifted censorship today from the country's leading daily newspaper and defender of press freedom. O Estado de São Paulo, which is celebrating its hundredth anniversary. Most other Brazilian newspapers obey orders not to print news

NEWSCASTER 2: considered offensive, such as student protests, strikes or the treatment of political prisoners. O Estado de São Paulo, which ignores these orders, has had censors in the composing room since August, 1972. These censors cut, erratically, anything they disliked. There was no announcement of the removal of censorship,

(NEWSCASTER 5 *lifts paper bags and* NEWSCASTERS 3 *and* 4 *mouth the news silently, very animated.*)

NEWSCASTER 2: but the newspaper appeared today with one hundred pages intact, without the columns of poetry used as fillers for censored material.

(NEWSCASTER 5 *replaces bags over heads of* NEWSCASTERS 3 *and* 4.)

NEWSCASTER 2: No one knows how long the censors will stay out of O Estado de São Paulo or whether this is a permanent or temporary measure.

(NEWSCASTER 5 *removes the paper bags.*)

NEWSCASTER 2: *(Pointedly, to* NEWSCASTERS 3 *and* 4) "It all depends, on the newspaper and how it reacts," one official said.

(NEWSCASTERS 3 *and* 4 *speak urgently, simultaneously.*)

NEWSCASTER 3: Some women find it hard to believe that their men had to go to Washington DC, Washington DC, I repeat, Wash—

NEWSCASTER 4: We had eyewitness reports that Brazilian torture police were trained in Washington DC, Washington DC, I repeat, Wash—

NEWSCASTER 5: Special from the Christian Century, October 22nd, 1975. Every Thursday afternoon, just before the paper is to go to press, the censor from the local police station arrives with his Magic Marker and stamp to censor the archdiocesan newspaper. When he has blotted out all offensive stories, opinions and editorials, poetry is inserted to fill the blank places. Thus all Brazilians enjoy classical culture with…what's left of the news…I mean what's right with the news… rather, the news that's fit to…still be in print.

NEWSCASTER 5: slides onto the news desk, turns his military hat backwards and transforms into a "captain kangaroo" character: big smiles, talking down to the audience as if they were children.

DANIELLE: I bought some camphor ice and moisturizing creams at Woolworths…

(NEWSCASTERS 3 *and* 4 *scream from beneath bags.*)

DANIELLE: …and I'm going on a very careful campaign to get my lips soft enough in winter so I won't chew them any more.

(*Censors*)

(NEWSCASTERS 2 *and* 5 *exit.* NEWSCASTERS 3 *and* 4, *relieved, remove their bags and take a big breath.*)

NEWSCASTER 3: Let's take a look at the weather on this nice day of (*Insert day of performance*) 20___. But before we do— "Now this!"

(NEWSCASTER 1 *is preparing herself to go on the air behind newscast desk right.* NEWSCASTER 5 *returns as a new personality and reclines on desk, attentive to her every word.)*

NEWSCASTER 1: How many voices do we deny every time we switch on T V?

NEWSCASTER 4: *(At newsdesk left)* Nestlé believes in Brazil!

NEWSCASTER 1: Our brains are overloaded.

NEWSCASTER 4: Mothers, save your moonlike beauty for your husbands. Feed your newborn Nestlé's Instant Balanced Baby Formula. *(Puts on red or blonde wig to give the Portuguese translation.)* Mães, guardem sua beleza lunada para o marido. Alimentem as crianças com a Proporcionada Receita Instantanea de Nestlé para bebés.

NEWSCASTER 1: We need a little gentle lulling.

(NEWSCASTER 2 *transforms into double agent, rushes in with a carrot and carrot shredder and hands it to* NEWSCASTER 5 *who's been lying face down on the desk.* NEWSCASTER 5 *starts madly shredding the carrot.)*

NEWSCASTER 1: Lie back on the bed with a great big steak…

(BARTON *lassoes* DANIELLE *with shower attachment.)*

NEWSCASTER 1: …and masturbate into your canteloupe.

(BARTON *pulls* DANIELLE *to his chest and holds her tight.)*

NEWSCASTER 4: Better than Mother and Nature can make. *(Melhor que podem fazer Mamãe e Natureza.)*

DANIELLE: *(Struggling)* It gives me visions of lip cancer.

NEWSCASTER 1: The seeds are sputtering. The seeds are spreading. The seeds are sucking out the seeds of your protein.

(BARTON *throws* DANIELLE *down so that her bottom is raised.*)

DANIELLE: What if it spread to my tongue?

(BARTON *calf-ropes* DANIELLE, *tying her two legs and one arm together with shower attachment.*)

NEWSCASTER 4: Easy instructions printed on every package in French, German, Spanish and Portuguese. *(Instrucções simples sobre cada pacote em francês, alemâo, espanhol e português.)*

NEWSCASTER 1: Mail your seeds to another galaxy. This solar system is about to regurgitate four trillion souls.

(*Completing the roping,* BARTON *lifts his arms to show he has completed the act.*)

DANIELLE: I'd kill myself.

NEWSCASTER 4: "If you can't read, improvise." (*"Se voce não pode ler, improvise."*)

DANIELLE: I'd kill myself.

(BARTON *demonstrates the possibilities of "fun" with a toilet plunger.*)

(NEWSCASTER 4 *transforms into a Brazilian* BEGGER WOMAN, NEWSCASTER 3 *into a* PIMP. *The* BEGGER WOMAN b*egins the line while the* PIMP *dips his fingers in red paint—the actor can make this look like he's snorting cocaine. Then he joins in with the* BEGGER WOMAN.)

BEGGAR WOMAN: The cost of living in Brazil has risen one thousand and thirty-seven percent over the last cost-of-living index in the Brazilin year of 1956.

(*The* PIMP *stomps the* BEGGER WOMAN, *scratches her face bloody with the red paint, then transforms into a sniper/* ASSASSIN *who climbs a rope, hanging over left news desk.*)

ASSASSIN: *(Climbing rope)* This is just a firm prod to get you moving. *(Grabs his crotch)* At Attica, laggards needed electricity.

(BARTON uses the plunger on DANIELLE's buttocks and thighs.)

DANIELLE: I used to try anything to get high…

(NEWSCASTERS 1, 4 and 5 transform into Brazilian peasants, who appear and dance with a DUPONT SPOKESWOMAN.)

DUPONT SPOKESWOMAN: *(NEWSCASTER 2, wearing a coolie hat)* DuPont believes in Brazil—and for years has been busy producing useful products for a growing population.

(BARTON uses the plunger:)

DANIELLE: …just so's I could put up with myself.

DUPONT SPOKESWOMAN: Products such as: Industrial explosives to help build roads…

(BARTON uses the plunger:)

DANIELLE: Sometimes it does get to be one of the hardest things there is…

DUPONT SPOKESWOMAN: …tunnels and dams.

(PEASANTS form a conga line and dance around her.)

DUPONT SPOKESWOMAN: DuPont is a leading supplier of X-ray films, herbicides and pesticides.

(BARTON uses the plunger:)

DANIELLE: …just to have to put up with being inside your own self.

(PEASANTS continue to dance around DUPONT SPOKESWOMAN—they begin to bump with her, move her around the playing area.)

DUPONT SPOKESWOMAN: Brazil has entered the decade of the 'Seventies…

(BARTON *uses the plunger:*)

DANIELLE: My Dad was the same way.

DUPONT SPOKESWOMAN: …with a program of inspiring national objectives.

(*The* PEASANTS *are getting rough in their dancing. they bump harder.* DUPONT SPOKESWOMAN *tries to maintain good relations, but aggressively bumps back.*)

(BARTON *uses the plunger:*)

DANIELLE: When I asked him why he got so drunk he used to tell me the same thing. He said it was just because he couldn't stand his own company.

DUPONT SPOKESWOMAN: DuPont is happy and proud to be part of the Brazilian scene and looks forward to making important contributions to Brazilian progress.

(*The aggressive dancing/bumping continues, getting more and more violent. They start to buzz. To create the insects and people, the actors should choose real lines to mumble.* NEWSCASTER 3 *enters as another DuPont person. He picks up* DUPONT SPOKESWOMAN *and using her as a large sprayer, sprays the* PEASANTS, *who cough and fall.*)

(*[*NEWSCASTER 1*] a* STUDENT *falls downstage center, coughing and holding her eyes as though she's been maced.once again, right before* DANIELLE *reaches a climax,* BARTON *stops using the plunger and walks away.* DANIELLE *unties herself.*)

DANIELLE: Somehow that made sense to me and I sort of forgave him.

STUDENT: (*Fighting to regain breath from having been maced*) And here's the way it is on May 10th, 1974. Today the powerful fifty-thousand-member Brazilian Bar Association issued a ten-point memorandum urging the military dictatorship to grant basic democratic and human freedoms to the people.

(NEWSCASTERS 2 *and 3 transform into police, who slowly pick her up and drag her toward the rope above news desk left where she will be strung up and tortured.*)

STUDENT: Among the rights and freedoms it demanded were: An independent judiciary; guarantees for human freedom; restoration of a fully operative habeas corpus; an end to secret arrests and the practice of holding accused persons incommunicado without charges; a halt to abduction of lawyers to pressure them into disclosing the whereabouts of their clients; and especially a halt to the practice of putting black hoods over the heads of interrogators.

(NEWSCASTER 5 *appears behind news desk left. police string* STUDENT *up on the rope and slowly proceed to break both her feet. As one policeman mimes breaking the foot, the other symbolically holds a 6" breaking stick and breaks it simultaneously with the foot breaking. repeat for each foot.* STUDENT *screams with each break.*)

NEWSCASTER 5: (*A straightforward news report*) We are confined in cells ten feet long

(*One foot is broken.*)

NEWSCASTER 5: and thirteen feet wide for twenty-three hours a day.

(*Other foot is broken.*)

(BARTON *brutally kneels* DANIELLE *on the chaise and places her arms behind her head, exposing the sides of her torso and breasts, then begins to demonstrate meat tenderizer on her body.*)

DANIELLE: I forget who I am once in a while.

(NEWSCASTER 4 *at desk right appears to be swallowing at the air.* NEWSCASTER 2 *huddles close to* NEWSCASTER 5.*)

NEWSCASTER 5: ...being allowed only one hour in the open air when there is sunshine.

(BARTON *uses meat tenderizer:*)

DANIELLE: I blend back into my Dad and I feel worse then than when I'm mad at myself.

(The STUDENT *turns herself on the rope and screams.)*

NEWSCASTER 5: Lights are kept on all night long,...

(BARTON *uses the meat tenderizer:*)

DANIELLE: I never seem to...

NEWSCASTER 5: ...aggravating...

(BARTON *uses the meat tenderizer:*)

DANIELLE: ...catch it at the time.

NEWSCASTER 5: ...three to a cell...

(BARTON *uses the meat tenderizer.*)

DANIELLE: I never sort it out when it's happening.

NEWSCASTER 5: ...relative deeply sacrifice to visit...

(BARTON *uses the meat tenderizer:*)

DANIELLE: I don't always realize it...

NEWSCASTER 5: *(Begins to experience the suffering, trying to fight it)* ...degradation...

(All NEWSCASTERS *pick up four-foot sticks and do isolated work on "prisoner under torture" images: an animal on a skewer, burning at the stake, etc. they must fight to rise above the pain of torture. the following lines are said during the torture images, no tears, only flat voices.*

PRISONER 5: *(Under torture)* ...and mutilation as human beings.

(BARTON *uses the meat tenderizer:*)

DANIELLE: ...it's after I been in some kind of long nightmare. I come out of this black, black sleep...

PRISONER 1: We are not allowed to work.

(BARTON *uses the meat tenderizr:)*

DANIELLE: …and there I am…

PRISONER 3: We have no work.

(BARTON *uses the meat tenderizer:)*

DANIELLE: …and I see it's me,…

PRISONER 1: We are forbidden to work.

(BARTON *uses the meat tenderizer:)*

DANIELLE: …I feel it's me,…

PRISONER 2: We cannot move, we cannot work, we are isolated.

(BARTON *uses the meat tenderizer:)*

DANIELLE: …but I feel like I been away from myself, not sure just where…

PRISONER 4: The imaginative and brilliantly trained guards…

(BARTON *uses the meat tenderizer:)*

DANIELLE: …but here I am back in the middle of me again,…

(BARTON *stops using the meat tenderizer.)*

PRISONER 4: …keep us under constant terror…

(NEWSCASTERS 1 *and* 5 *drop torture images and move to news desk right—the others continue torture images.* NEWSCASTER 1 *transforms into a sophisticated, high-fashion* PARIS REPORTER, NEWSCASTER 5 *into the* FINANCE MINISTER.)

PARIS REPORTER: Paris, special from *Le Monde,* May 24th, 1970: Brazilian Finance Minister admitted to Marcel Niedergang of Le Monde that…

FINANCE MINISTER: The use of torture is very prejudicial to our world-wide economic progress and the improvement of our financial system… We believe that economic expansion will solve our internal social problems, but to bring this about, we still need three or four years of social stability at home.

PARIS REPORTER: And that means keeping anti-social personalities and groups in the state cooler?

FINANCE MINISTER: Only for three or four more years.

DANIELLE: …and I feel very…

(PARIS REPORTER *and* FINANCE MINISTER *take beat of five,* PRISONERS *simultaneously look front and drop their sticks, and all whisper together.*)

ALL NEWSCASTERS: …psychic disturbances.

DANIELLE: (BARTON *uses the meat tenderizr.*) …very shaky.

(All NEWSCASTERS *except number 4 Transform into members of the dictatorship, choose various images in which to use their sticks to torture* PRISONER 4.)

PRISONER 4: We find it imperative to mention the names of some of our cellmates who have been thrown into solitary confinement; dark, humid, unhealthy cells, kept for months Sebastião Medeiros Filho; Eleuteuio Aluisio; Regina Sarmanjo; Ferreira Palmar; Sebastião Cornelio. The last two went mad and were shot.

(All turn forward and break their "breaking sticks". NEWSCASTERS 3 *and* 5 *transform into* SINGERS *and dance among the* PRISONERS. *Other* NEWSCASTERS *dance with their sticks as backup for the* SINGERS. *One does the limbo, one does a seductive dance, one waltzes.*)

SINGERS: *(Sing)* Hey, hey, ain't we all Americans under the skin? Hey baby, let me in. I can't wait to get it in. Ya know in your heart we is all just plain old Americans under our skin. Hah, hah hah, hah.

(This line done with breath only—faces in fixed smiles—no tone—hands palm-open to audience.)

*(*BARTON *sponges* DANIELLE*'s entire body with a wet scouring sponge during her next speech.)*

DANIELLE: So I often wonder just what it is I want from myself.

(All NEWSCASTERS *quickly place their torture sticks in an irregular pattern on the floor and each walk their stick as if it were a life-or-death tightrope walk. then they transform into elementary* TEACHERS, *using other sticks to point with.)*

TEACHER 2: This statement I want to share with you children, comes from a primary resource group of what are known in the adult world as "political prisoners."

(As each TEACHER *completes his/her statement, [s]he continues to repeat emblems of it under the other speeches. focus in on the* TEACHER *who speaks for the first time.)*

DANIELLE: I wonder how I'm supposed to feel.

TEACHER 5: This means that some of the people are separated away from most of the people.

DANIELLE: How is anybody supposed to feel good all by herself?

TEACHER 3: They are arrested, usually very early in the morning while still asleep, beaten and taken to an island off the coast of Brazil near Rio.

DANIELLE: Completely by herself.

TEACHER 1: That's Rio de Janeiro. Who can find it on the map?

*(*TEACHERS *jam with key words and phrases from their individual speeches—e g:)*

TEACHER 1: ...political prisoners...

TEACHER 5: Some…separated…most…

TEACHER 3: …arrested early…beaten…taken…

TEACHER 4: That's Rio…Rio…)

(BARTON *resumes yoga and breathing exercises.*)

(*All* TEACHERS/NEWSCASTERS *back up on stick as if suddenly frightened, then pick up their sticks and move off stage.* NEWSCASTER 4 *rushes in down the center of the playing area, giving a wild Latin call "ahy yay yah yay!"* NEWSCASTERS 1 *and* 2 *begin slowly swinging their sticks on either side of her so she must jump over them. these are violent actions but have dance discipline.*)

NEWSCASTER 4: My friend Maria, black-sleek, and playfully dangerous, When she wasn't seducing Ambassadors, Lived in a Brazilian palace as a small child And watched her uncle dictate and Learned how to drink herself To death.

(NEWSCASTERS 1 *and* 2 *hit their sticks together in front of* NEWSCASTER *and begin to dance aggressive fencing moves at her, slicing at her. she relates to them as dance partners.*)

NEWSCASTER 4: Last year at the age of thirty-six, She threw up her liver all over her hospital gown. Her sobbing Mama wiped her withered chin With a satin sheet embroidered in Monarchical laughter and cried and cried—

(NEWSCASTER 1 *and* 2 *hit sticks together in front of her.*)

NEWSCASTER 4: At her husband for not being serious.

(NEWSCASTERS 1 and 2 violently swing their sticks above her head as if to decapitate her—she ducks and avoids contact.

NEWSCASTER 4: He had been occupied with peddling coffee futures to lobbyists In Washington. His Mercedes-Benz was two years old And no one would loan him money any more.

(NEWSCASTERS 1 and 2 stand at attention left and right of stage with their sticks like staffs.

NEWSCASTER 4: *(Quietly)* When we looked in the door, Maria laughed, *(Laughs as Maria)* and the old Sexual fire lit up her huge black eyes and she said just above the death rattle, *(Transforms into Maria and laughs at all of them)* You'll never find the map. I hid the map that shows where I hid all the money. I ate the map that shows where I saw all the money hidden. I ate the map that shows where all the money is hidden. *(Bitterly)* The money inflated from the hides of my people in Brazil. *(Frivolously)* That is the latest poop and the last peep that you'll Ever hear from me. I'm leaving you all to join Road Runner and Crusader Rabbit. Television was my sloth in life and Will be my solace in death.

(Pause—two sticks crack together)

NEWSCASTER 4: *(As herself again)* She disappeared into her tummy T V And I never heard Maria's voice again.

(NEWSCASTER 2 *slowly and tenderly places stick behind* NEWSCASTER 4*'s knees and leads her downstage left.* NEWSCASTER 1 *uses the stick to break* NEWSCASTER 4*'s back as if with the "iron bed".)*

(Also done tenderly)

(NEWSCASTER 4 *Reacts to the pain silently in slow motion.)*

(Simultaneously, DANIELLE *begins her speech and* BARTON *demonstrates the fuzzy bottle cleaner.)*

DANIELLE: Completely by herself, without any booze or pills or smokes or coffee or tea or malted milks, or sweet air, or the radio, or…

(BARTON t*hrows* DANIELLE o*nto the chaise on her back with the bottle cleaners clenched in his teeth, hoists up her knees, then thrusts the bottle cleaner between her legs—changing rhythms, teasing, slowing to a stop, resuming. The television area is silent during the beginning of this thrusting.*

She cries out with pleasure. When NEWSCASTER 4 *[as*
TEACHER*] begins speaking,* BARTON *continues thrusting,*
but he and DANIELLE *are quieter.)*

(In television area, scene transforms to a Brazilian jail cell
where all the NEWSCASTERS *are confined. Each selects*
a torture image using stick. Conditions are crowded, all
inmates seem connected by the sticks, all are on their guard,
working with isolated eye movements.)

NEWSCASTER 4: *(As* TEACHER—*intimately, watching to*
see no guards enter or are within earshot) A friend of mine
sent me a copy of the letter the prisoners sent to the
world. These people only had the floor to write on.
One political prisoner played the part of lookout while
another crouched on the stone floor to write. Every
time a guard came by, the paper had to be hidden
under a dead rat. Here are some of the things the
prisoners…

(She wanted to finish by saying "…wanted to say to the free
world," but is interrupted. BARTON *stops thrusting bottle*
cleaner exactly when teacher stops speaking. He goes to
exercise. NEWSCASTER 3 *comes forward through the mass*
of prisoners as the MANAGEMENT REPRESENTATIVE *and*
addresses the T V Camera and audience. NEWSCASTERS 1
and 2 transform into guerillas and swing their sticks in slow
motion like heavy clubs.)

MANAGEMENT REPRESENTATIVE: *(Warm announcer*
approach) This is the only time the sponsors will
interrupt this program about the terrible things going
on in Brazil. We feel it's more important for you the
public to be aware of the terrible tortures going on in
Brazil than to be interrupted all the time by commercial
messages.

*(*NEWSCASTER 1 *[*MANAGEMENT REPRESENTATIVE*] and 2*
hit him behind the knees—he falls in slow motion)

MANAGEMENT REPRESENTATIVE: We'll keep our message short as a riding crop,

(NEWSCASTERS 1 *and* 2 *slowly bring one stick over his head to his teeth as he completes the line.*)

MANAGEMENT REPRESENTATIVE: tight as a bit in your teeth.

(*As he spits out the sticks, he comes to his feet and instantly transforms into a suave, but slightly fly-by-night* SALESPERSON, *in black-rimmed glasses with a Brazilian bird perched over one ear. An* ATTENDANT [NEWSCASTER 2] *shuffles in and presents to him, on a small pillow, a suspendered jockstrap which the* SALESPERSON *pulls on to advertise "obedience" magazine.* ATTENDANT *shuffles off. Two more* ATTENDANTS [NEWSCASTERS 1 *and* 2] *crawl backwards to center stage.*)

SALESPERSON: (*Friendly but high-pressure*) Subscribed now to Obedience, an S and M extravaganza!

(BARTON *demonstrates a feather duster.*)

(DANIELLE *seduces* BARTON *who continues his demonstration:*)

DANIELLE: I think I've figured out why I turn on the water tap or flush the john when I go to the bathroom. It isn't 'cause I'm embarrassed to pee.

SALESPERSON: Humiliation, spanking, bondage, only fifty dollars for a six-month trial offer.

DANIELLE: (*With an eye on* BARTON) Everyone, no matter who, has to take a pee. I turn on the water to confuse my enemies.

SALESPERSON: (*Noticing the two* ATTENDANTS) For me, the sight of a pair of submissive buttocks…

DANIELLE: (*On hands and knees*) That's right.

SALESPERSON: (*Sits on* ATTENDANTS' *shoulders*) … quivering and squirming beneath the stroke of my whip or the sting of my open palm, creates within me an intense thrilling passion.

(BARTON *uses feather duster on* DANIELLE—*it tickles—she reacts. Sometimes it gets so intense she moves away—this makes him angry.*)

DANIELLE: Same things as my dog trying to bury his crap. So's no one knows you been this way.

SALESPERSON: It does not overwhelm me.

(BARTON *uses feather duster:*)

DANIELLE: We got a lot of hangovers walking a round with us.

SALESPERSON: I am controlled and efficient in administering corporal punishment, (*Leaping up*) but I am moved—physically, intellectually and emotionally—from just one of the exciting eyewitness accounts.

DANIELLE: That's one of them.

(*The two* ATTENDANTS *crawl forward between his legs:*)

SALESPERSON: Our magazine *Sado-Macho Blue* is a unique publication strictly for the S and M fan…

DANIELLE: Someone tracking you and hearing you pee…

(SALESPERSON *squeezes the two* ATTENDANTS, *who respond:*)

SALESPERSON: …contains quality bondage and discipline fiction,…

DANIELLE: …would know right where to get you.

(SALESPERSON *gives two kicks to the side—the two* ATTENDANTS *fly out as if kicked and land right and left of stage, motionless.*)

SALESPERSON: …"how-to-beat-it" articles…

DANIELLE: That's where the expression "getting caught with yer pants down" comes from.

SALESPERSON: …serialized discipline novels,…

(BARTON *uses feather duster:*)

DANIELLE: A member from another tribe, a guy from another gang could pick you right off.

SALESPERSON: …unusual "letters to the editor"…

(BARTON *tracks* DANIELLE *with duster in his mouth, then holds it behind his head like a savage headdress:*)

DANIELLE: An animal can even smell the saliva in your mouth; that's why yer mouth gets dry when yer scared. (*Runs over and around chaise as if scared of* BARTON)

SALESPERSON: …i. e., "Blonde master with good muscle definition, cruel and merciless temperment, seeks rich, docile slaves."

(BARTON, *infuriated by the "play" chase, stops and resumes exercises, or pretends to.*)

DANIELLE: (*Keeps running as if being chased*) Can you imagine in the old days one of those dinosaurs or brontosauruses chasing the hell out of you just because it caught a whiff of your breath?

SALESPERSON: Search no more, discipline devotees.

DANIELLE: You'd be a goner without even taking a pee. You see?

SALESPERSON: (*Crossing to* ATTENDANT *right, shaking her*) Subscribe now, get a free bonus.

DANIELLE: You see, nearly everything has a reason to it…

SALESPERSON: (*Crossing to* ATTENDANT *left and slapping her*) Sign your name,…

DANIELLE: …if you think about it logically.

SALESPERSON: *(Crosses back to* ATTENDANT *right, tries to rouse her)* ...certify under penalty of perjury you are over twenty-one years of age...

DANIELLE: But sometimes I get so rattled,...

SALESPERSON: *(Crosses to* ATTENDANT *left and squeezes)* ...send you a free brochure of delicious bondage devices and forward your name to the erotic category of your choice.

DANIELLE: ...even if I haven't seen anyone in days,...

SALESPERSON: *(To audience) Sado-Macho Blue* is fifty dollars for a six-month trial.

DANIELLE: ...that I can't settle down...

SALESPERSON: *(Removes jockstrap and aggressively throws it down)* Submit—your check!

DANIELLE: ...to think about anything.

(NEWSCASTER *scene transforms to a busy Brazilian street scene.* NEWSCASTERS *transform to Brazilian citizens and students, exhausted from their protest efforts, marching back and forth with banners, leaflets and signs, chanting, "guerga".)*

(BARTON *selects the turkey baster and demonstrates this suction device on* DANIELLE's *breasts, ass, nose, etc. She responds with pleasure-pain, sighing and crying throughout.)*

(NEWSCASTER 4 *emerges from the group wearing a hard hat and begins to interview the* PROTESTERS, *directing microphone to record all audible statements, including screams on being maced or raped, or repeated lines like "dictatorship".)*

NEWSCASTER 4: *(As* REPORTER*)* Here are some of the things the prisoners wanted to say to the Free World...

PROTESTER 1: *(Proud but weak)* To the International Commission on Human Rights; to the free people of the world; to all institutions that struggle for justice and freedom…

(PROTESTER 1 *throws a nail-studded golf ball*—PROTESTER 5 *[A* STUDENT*] catches it and sinks to the ground, repeating, "…struggle for justice".)*

PROTESTER 3: *(Brave but weak)* Our voices rise above the electrodes and the torture racks of the Brazilian dictatorship…

(A COP *[*NEWSCASTER 2*] maces* PROTESTER 1, *who sinks to the floor screaming:)*

PROTESTER 1: Dictatorship!

PROTESTER 5: *(Proud but weak)* …true facts…life of political prisoners…Brazilian military regime…since 1964…we struggle…

(A COP *[*NEWSCASTER 3*] maces* PROTESTER 1, *who screams and collapses.)*

PROTESTER 2: *(Bravely)* …misery…exploitation of…

(A COP *[*NEWSCASTER 5*] maces* PROTESTER 2 *who collapses.)*

PROTESTER 3: …Brazilian people…

*(*BARTON *stops using the turkey baster.)*

NEWSCASTER 4: *(To audience, as* REPORTER*)* And now our weekly feature "Know When You've Been Attacked," related and demonstrated by eyewitness attackees.

*(*BARTON *begins demonstrating plant mister to the beat of the music.)*

(Rock 'n roll duet: PROTESTER 1 *recovers from being maced center stage and transforms into a* STUDENT *stage right,* PROTESTER 3 *also becomes a* STUDENT, *stage left. First two introductions are spoken. The other* NEWSCASTERS *are at the two news desks—they play percussion instruments and*

*perform as a paralyzed backup group, moving into paralysis
images during the choruses.)*

STUDENT: I'm Rosalie T. I was maced. It was in
Washington, DC. On May Day, 1970. I was trying to
help the cops. Some people were sitting in the street…

STUDENT 3: I'm Allan M. I was gassed In Berkeley on
the way To the laundromat On October 17, 1968.

(STUDENT 1 falls in image of covering eyes.)

STUDENT 3: *(Sings and dances)* It knocked me off
my feet. It knocked me off my feet. They were
carrying Double tanks on their backs, The kind with a
hose and nozzle. He had this nozzle In his hand And
pointed it Straight at me. I was at the laundromat
door. He squirted the gas And I couldn't move any
more.

*(STUDENT 3 crosses arms to protect face, does I Ching
isolations during STUDENT 1's verse.)*

STUDENT: *(Sings and dances)*
I had my gas mask with me,
But I couldn't get it up to
Protect my face
Before I got the mace.
I was trying to get people out of the street
When this cop pressed his top and went bop bop bop…
(Falls in "mace" image)

STUDENT 3: *(Sings and dances)*
I was trying to get in
When they fried my skin.
One shot of gas
And they fried my ass,
Burning all over.
I went right down,
Down to the ground,
To the ground.

STUDENTS 1 & 3: *(Singing and dancing together)*
I realized I was paralyzed,
I realized I was paralyzed.

*(*CHORUS *sings with them.)*

STUDENTS 1 & 3 *and* CHORUS:
I tried to protected my eyes.

STUDENT:
Come on you guys, get out of the street.
Don't provoke the cops.
Then there we were,
Me and this mace,
Face to face.
He went for my eyes,
He went for my eyes,
My eyes,
My eyes,
My eyes,
My eyes.

STUDENTS 1 & 3 *and* CHORUS:
I realized I was paralyzed,
I realized I was paralyzed,
I realized I was paralyzed,
I realized I was paralyzed,
But my friends saved my eyes,
My eyes,
My eyes.

*(*STUDENTS 1 *and* 3 *fall to floor itching, holding eyes,
repeating their individual mace images. Then* NEWSCASTER
1 *rises and gives temperature center stage.)*

NEWSCASTER 1: The temperature in *(City in which play is
performed)* is *(actual current temperature)* degrees.

*(*BARTON *uses plant mister [(rhythmically, like a musical
instrument] on* DANIELLE's *breasts, her thighs and
especially her face.)*

(As BARTON *uses plant mister:)*

DANIELLE: When I'm almost asleep, I've taken to trying to watch my mind go by. It's a new thing. It's a really nice thing. The thing is that it's been going on all my life, at least at least as long as my mind has been into words.

*(*NEWSCASTER 2 *appears center stage. during her announcement* NEWSCASTER 5 *transforms into* REVEREND MORRIS, *who comes forward beside her, smiles and nods.* NEWSCASTERS 1 *and* 3, *in the torture area stage right, select torture images and move [e. g., pulling out fingernails, threatening burns with a lighted cigar] forward and back in slow motion, their faces stoic throughout.)*

NEWSCASTER 2: And now the headlines. "Tortured Missionary says U S supports terrorists." In an exclusive interview in the *Omaha World-Herald,* June 17th, 1975, the Reverend Frederick B Morris, Methodist missionary to Brazil, said…

REVEREND MORRIS: *(Standing in profile center stage holding cross on his back, smiling graciously, speaking to his congregation)* I was imprisoned and tortured for seventeen days.

*(*NEWSCASTER 2 *rises slowly center stage, spotlit if possible, and begins to sing to audience. Other* NEWSCASTERS *join* NEWSCASTERS 1 *and* 4 *stage right and slump with mouths hanging like idiots.)*

*(*BARTON *continues to use plant mister on* DANIELLE—*she responds. this begins to look like a wet disco number as backup to the song.)*

NEWSCASTER 2: *(Sings)* Can this really happen To human men and women? You'd need a hundred thousand men To torture fifty thousand. How can it happen? How can it happen? You can't brainwash an entire people To torture their own. No animal is so consciously cruel As to burn flesh—break bones. It can't be true. How can it happen?

NEWSCASTER 1: *(Sings and makes isolated gestures of a commandant on each phrase. Clicks heels and comes to attention in unison with* NEWSCASTERS 3, 4 *and* 5*)* Out of fear,

*(*NEWSCASTER 1 *lunges forward in unison with* NEWSCASTERS 3, 4 *and* 5.*)*

NEWSCASTER 1: Out of fear,

(They turn somersaults in unison.)

NEWSCASTER 1: Because of patriotism, my dear.

(They turn in circles as dogs chasing tails.)

NEWSCASTER 1: They're just doing their job to control the misled mob.

(They sit on floor, jaws hanging.)

NEWSCASTER 1: We go berserk Listening to some Red-brained jerk.

*(*NEWSCASTERS 3, 4 *and* 5 *march upstage left on hands and feet, bellies up, like ants, and sing:)*

ALL: They'll never call me Nero
(March in place)
In my country's uniform.
(March left)
When I turn the thumbscrew
I do so as a hero.

NEWSCASTER 2: *(Crosses to embrace* NEWSCASTER 1, *who rejects her)* In all reality

*(*NEWSCASTER 2 *crosses to embrace* NEWSCASTER 3, *who rejects her.)*

NEWSCASTER 2: Nowadays I can't believe

*(*NEWSCASTER 2 *crosses to embrace* NEWSCASTER 4, *who rejects her.)*

NEWSCASTER 2: Human beings can lose all sensibility,

(Crosses to embrace NEWSCASTER 5, *who rejects her)*

NEWSCASTER 2:
And give themselves over to such blind cruelty.

OTHERS: *(Form diagonal line, flagellate selves as they sing)*
It is vital
To put down fear,
To protect all
We hold dear
(Arms to the heavens)
From wild-eyed
Terrorist bands
(Slowly drop to knees)
Who would destroy
With joy
(Offer audience a gift)
Our fatherland.

NEWSCASTER 4: *(Rises, crosses to* NEWSCASTER 2, *stage right, doing a Spanish dance)*
Think of the Spanish Inquisition,
Those souls possessed
By the devil. Fire burned brighter than the sun. A goal
to save each soul, *(Seducing* NEWSCASTER 2*)* Torture
was seen as a salvation.

NEWSCASTER 1: *(Coming forward center stage)* Through
the research of recent sages
We've learned nine million
Women were burned at the stake
For their own sake.

*(*NEWSCASTER 1 *crosses to* NEWSCASTER 3, NEWSCASTER
4 *rises and crosses to* NEWSCASTER 5, *they "lay hands" on
them.)*

NEWSCASTER 1: In the Middle Ages
These women had knowledge of healing,
But to purify them

(NEWSCASTER 3 *lifts* NEWSCASTER 1, NEWSCASTER 5 *lifts*
NEWSCASTER 4, *they carry them to news desks right and
left.* NEWSCASTERS 3 *and* 5 *get candles, give them to* 1, 2,
and 4.)

NEWSCASTER 1: They piled on the wood
Until their skin was peeling.

(NEWSCASTER 1 *and* NEWSCASTER 4 *slowly float off desks
and come downstage with candles*—NEWSCASTER 2 *crosses
to center stage between them.*)

NEWSCASTER 1: Black as the smoke
That clouded the ruling
Mind—but nothing is really
Lost, my dear—
But nothing is really lost.
Out of fear
Their knowledge was
Gone for a time
But in our enlightened clime
We are rediscovering
All that the burned witches
Once knew about herbal healing.

(NEWCASTER 1 *and* NEWSCASTER 4 *blow out their candles,
turn to* NEWSCASTER 2 *and push her to the floor, into the
audience.*)

(NEWSCASTER 1 *hops and nods "yes" with* NEWSCASTERS
3, 4, *and* 5:)

NEWSCASTER 1: The fire gagged Them for Four
hundred years.

(They shake their heads "yes" and "no," confused.)

NEWSCASTER 1: The righteous found Their
righteousness was as rags.

(Shrugging isolations)

NEWSCASTER 1: But they did it, And they did it out of fear, My dear.

NEWSCASTER 2: *(Rises, comes back on stage)* I still can't believe human beings Can turn into friends And then back again.

OTHERS: *(Big show-stopper finale dance)*
It's not a matter of sin.
Hannah said, "Evil is banal,
That's all."
Look within—don't lag.
Look within—don't lag.
Do the Righteous Rag,
Do the Righteous Roll,
Do the Righteous Rock.
Close your eyes—hide your soul.
Close your eyes—hide your soul.

(NEWSCASTERS 1, 3, 4 and 5 come together in a tight group upstage center and speak in rhythm:)

NEWSCASTERS 1, 3, 4 & 5: *(Self-righteously)* Ho ho ho, I'm holier than those. *(Standing stoically)* Ho ho ho, who's holier than thou?

NEWSCASTER 2: *(Takes over again, stopping the show)* I don't believe it's going on and I'm not going to report it any more.

NEWSCASTER 3: *(Crosses nonchalantly to news desk right)* What you getting so excited about? All you have to do is read the news.

NEWSCASTER 2: *(Desperate)* I can't be sure it's the truth.

NEWSCASTER 4: *(Runs up to her, giggling)* You can't be sure you are even here— *(Runs around to her other side. Giggling:)* —why do you care what you read? *(Runs around stage, giggling)*

NEWSCASTER 2: *(Grabs and stops* NEWSCASTER 4*)* I'm a responsible, moral person.

NEWSCASTER 5: *(Nonchalantly at news desk left)* Who likes to get your paycheck every week.

NEWSCASTER 2: *(Crossing to* NEWSCASTER 5*)* Money doesn't mean that much to me.

NEWSCASTER 1: *(Stage right)* Then quit.

NEWSCASTER 2: *(Crossing to* NEWSCASTER 1*)* All right. I will. I quit.

*(*NEWSCASTER 1 *is joined by all the others in reaching out to* NEWSCASTER 2*, touching her, ruffling her hair, persuading her:)*

NEWSCASTER 1: Hey, I was only kidding—we got a nice group here. We get along fine—don't quit. Come on, try a new hairstyle, take your mind off questions.

NEWSCASTER 2: *(Struggles)* No. I'm going to quit in protest. I'm going to tell the management, I can't read news I don't trust. I don't believe human beings can be so cruel to other human beings—not without some sort of reason.

NEWSCASTER 1: I told you the reason. *(Tenderly squeezing* NEWSCASTER 2*'s shoulders, supporting her, trying to reach her)* They are torturing common rabble-rousers, who are nothing but mugger terrorists, who like to pop off kneecaps and kidnap Ambassadors and heads of American corporation… they hold them for ransom, or they knock off banks to further their popular people's struggles. It's necessary to torture these fools. They expect it. What else would they have to hold up to the so-called "masses" to cry about?

(The touching gets stronger, forcing NEWSCASTER 2 *to the ground.)*

NEWSCASTER 1: Repression, oppression, persecution. It's the same old story.

NEWSCASTER 2: *(On her knees, instantly recovers)* I'll jar the management, I'll wake them up. I haven't missed a day at work since I started. But this is too much! They'll wake up when I quit.

(All shrug:)

NEWSCASTER 1: They'll get another one just like you. What are you, crazy? This is a good job, and you get high recognition factor in the streets.

(They group together and put on "newspersonality")

NEWSCASTER 2: *(Stands, takes the line bravely to audience)* I'm fond of you all, but I'm leaving. I must protect my ideals about human beings. *(To* NEWSCASTERS*)* I'll miss you. *(To audience)* I'll miss you. *(Turns upstage, emotionally embraces other* NEWSCASTERS, *then exits)*

NEWSCASTER 5: We didn't even get to have a good-bye party.

(All show disappointment.)

NEWSCASTER 3: That's a Pisces for you.

NEWSCASTER 2: *(Re-enters wearing blonde wig)* Hello, I'm the new newscaster. Which desk is mine?

(They push NEWSCASTER 2 *here and there, finally seating her behind news desk left:)*

NEWSCASTER 3: This one.

NEWSCASTER 4: Here.

NEWSCASTER 1: You're on the air.

(During the following speech the other NEWSCASTERS *transform into Brazilian indians, who run as if through underbrush in different areas over entire playing area, calling and answering one another with Brazilian percussion instruments.)*

(BARTON *sprays* DANIELLE *even more violently. As she begins to reach climax, he leaves, only to return and leave again.)*

NEWSCASTER 2: *(Reading with smile to camera, totally uninvolved in what she's reading)* Nineteen seventy-four, April. The Bertrand Russell Two Tribunal on Latin America released a provisional verdict of South American government violation of human rights. The prime violators are identified as Brazil and Chile. Under the heading, "Establishment of the Facts," the paper says " The Tribunal possesses a list of more than a thousand people who have been tortured in Brazil. It also has a list of the torturers and a description of the very refined means that are used, as well as a detailed information about the public offices, commissariats and barracks where torture is practiced. It is difficult to describe in a few phrases all the atrocious systems used to create maximum suffering in the victims. All the possible means of pressure—physical, psychological and moral—are used, with increasing sophistication, by specialists whose imagination surpasses that of Dante. This is no exaggeration, for as far as we know, no children were tortured in the poet's "Hell." In Brazil, there was a case of a one-year-old baby who was given electric shocks in the presence of her father. One witness referred to the case of a lawyer who was tortured together with his six-year-old daughter, and that of a child of three tortured in the presence of his mother. The torture machines have been highly perfected. One of them is made in North America."

DANIELLE: …four, three, two, one. That almost always works. But this other night I was almost asleep and saying "four, three, two, one" …this piece of sentence floated past my eye, or my ear…well, it's hard to know which it is when you're in that nice state between being awake and halfway asleep.

DANIELLE: This phrase said, "Suck assassination via malted milk straw."

(BARTON *leaves* DANIELLE *abruptly and exercises—this is the end of their play with water)*

NEWSCASTER 1: *(A la Walter Cronkite—appearing stage right and casually walking downstage)* And here's the way it is, ladies and gentlemen, on April 20th, 1974. Five members of that popular theatre group, the Teatro oficina, were arrested in São Paulo, allegedly for possession of drugs.

DANIELLE: It woke me up.

NEWSCASTER 1: Besides being charged with drug possession...

DANIELLE: It woke me up all the way.

NEWSCASTER 1: ...the Oficina troupe is also being indicted for crimes against the National Security Law.

DANIELLE: I lay there in bed,...

NEWSCASTER 1: *(Gravely, trying to fight back gales of laughter)* The crime the members of the theatre troupe committed is very grave.

DANIELLE: ...my eyes wide open, I heard myself say it out loud. *(She is shocked by the image she sees.)*

NEWSCASTER 1: *(Solemnly)* They sold copies of a poster showing U S A President Nixon dressed as a prisoner.

DANIELLE: "Suck assassination via malted milk straw." *(Pause—she recovers.)* Then this weird thing happened inside my head. All the knots that had been there for days untied themselves, and the next thing I knew it was morning. I'm looking forward to tonight. It's causing me to be more careful with myself.

(NEWSCASTER 5 *breaks a "breaking stick" at news desk right.)*

NEWSCASTER 4: *(At news desk left, in announcer persona)*
"Clamps are placed on torture tools." Here's the
way it is Monday, May 8th, 1978. Special from the
Washington Bureau of United Press International to the
Omaha World-Herald— *(Transforms into a woman gossip
columnist)* Congress has taken steps to prohibit the
export of thumbscrews, leg irons, shackles and electric
shock batons to governments that engage in gross
violations of human rights. Representative Donald
Fraser, Democrat of Minnesota, said, *(Transforms into
Donald Fraser, who is constantly exasperated, shakes his
head and waves his arms)* "I find it incredible that these
torture instruments from the Dark Ages are still being
manufactured, let alone exported abroad." *(Transforms
back to gossip comumnist)* Again, that date is May 9th,
1978.

DANIELLE: I used to plan a lot to do very active things.
Very, very active things. One of my favorite things
to do was to camp out on the Peninsula. *(Swings and
jumps off upper platform into brazil/news area and sings,
flapping her arms and moving around playing area like a
bird)*
I've always lived in the North.
I've never been South.
I love to stay in bed when it's cold
(Crosses back to upper platform and BARTON*)*
And hold the South in my mouth.

BARTON: *(Sings and beats at* DANIELLE *in time with music)*
Repetition is balm for my soul—
Fifty piano-playing women
In an underwater glow,
A thousand pair of legs.

DANIELLE: I can go anywhere without getting out of
bed— *(Jumps onto* BARTON*'s back)*
Conquer with Eric the Red,
Skip up Everest without a climb,

Make time stand still,
Or at my will,
Expand into a galaxie.

(BARTON *crosses to front of chaise lifts* DANIELLE *across his shoulders, her body stiff, crosses downstage and spins with her.*)

BARTON: Time lapse into
One human blossom
Photographed through a lamé filter
(*Puts her down*)
From the point of view
Of Dick Powell's big toe.
(*Spoken, flexing his muscles and posing*)
What a show!
What a show!
What a show!
(*Spoken simultaneously with* DANIELLE's *next line as he chases her half-heartedly*)
I'm in love with you, Busby Berkeley!

(DANIELLE *sings while play-running from* BARTON, *who soon returns to muscle-flexing:*)

DANIELLE: In one drop I'm in the jungle, Chattering with chimpanzees. When I come back (*Crosses to chaise*) I'll come with a fin. I've decided in my next life To come back as a dolphin. (*She transforms into a teenybopper star-worshipper, throws herself at his feet, moves closer to him with each line he sings.*)

BARTON: (*Strong-man pose center stage*)
And oh the bananas,
(*Another strong-man pose*)
And oh the bananas,
(*Another*)
And oh the bananas.
(*Opening seducing to audience*)
worn and played by Carmen Miranda.

(Crosses to left of upper platform)
Next to Busby you are my ideal.
(Pulls himself into chair and lunges)
To me you are the epitome of all that was real.
I want to go the way you Went,
Ascend to heaven tapping to "Tico Tico"
On four hundred crescent moons,
(Stands in front of chaise, begins beating his thigh with mop head) The star of my own Banana show.

(DANIELLE, still on floor in Brazil/T V area, looks at BARTON, looks away, starts to walk out on him, looks back at him, repeats this three times during musical interlude before her verse. when she starts to sing, she crosses up to him, cradles herself inside his standing legs.)

DANIELLE:
I've always lived in the North. I've never been South.
(Snuggling in)
I love to stay in bed when it's cold
And hold the South in my mouth.
(Looks up at his crotch, snaps at it with her teeth)

(BARTON exercises.)

(NEWSCASTER 1 appears as COMMERCIAL ANNOUNCER sitting on news desk right wearing bird-covered hardhat, NEWSCASTER 2 appears as DU PONT REPRESENTATIVE standing in torture area right with two long sticks.)

COMMERCIAL ANNOUNCER: Shell believes in Brazil.

DU PONT REPRESENTATIVE: DuPont believes in Brazil.

DANIELLE: I'd lay awake for hours listing the items I'd take in my pack… *(Lists them in her head)*

(COMMERCIAL ANNOUNCER rises, DU PONT REPRESENTATIVE places the two sticks over both their shoulders. All NEWSCASTERS transform into the following torture image NEWSCASTER 4 starts moving from behind

*desk right—*NEWSCASTER 3 *knocks her out, slits her throat,
hoists her and* NEWSCASTER 5 *onto sticks. this image is
slowly walked across the playing area.* NEWSCASTER 3
*barks at the processional like a hungry dog. Musician or one
of the* NEWSCASTERS *blows whistle in samba rhythm, all*
NEWSCASTERS *move quickly to desks, scene transforms into
their food break—we see just their heads.)*

(All but NEWSCASTER 2 *gobble the food directly from the
desks.)*

NEWSCASTER 1: Aren't you going to eat your dinner?

NEWSCASTER 2: *(Pushing imaginary food away)* I ate my
mashed potatoes.

NEWSCASTER 3: *(Replacing it in front of her)* You have to
eat more than that.

NEWSCASTER 4: You can't work as hard as we do on
mashed potatoes.

NEWSCASTER 2: *(Pushing plate away)* I'm full.

NEWSCASTER 3: *(Replacing plate in front of her)* Eat some
more.

NEWSCASTER 2: I hate liver.

NEWSCASTER 1: Give liver a chance.

*(*NEWSCASTER 2 *makes gagging sound, continues till her
next line.)*

NEWSCASTER 1: Eat, so we can go back to work.

NEWSCASTER 2: *(Jumps up, ready)* I'm ready to work.

NEWSCASTER 5: *(Crosses to* NEWSCASTER 2, *settles her back
down at table)* The liver is delicious. They cooked it with
bacon and onions in butter.

NEWSCASTER 2: Nitrates, nitrites, saturated fats.
Ugggghhhhhh!

NEWSCASTER 1: Come on and clean your plate.

NEWSCASTER 5: You can't deliver news on an empty stomach.

NEWSCASTER 4: *(Holding her nose)* Hold you nose like this and chew. You'll get used to it.

NEWSCASTER 2: I'll never get used to liver.

NEWSCASTER 3: Eat it up now.

NEWSCASTER 4: Don't be a baby.

NEWSCASTER 5: *(Whispers)* Can I have your onions?

NEWSCASTER 1: If you don't eat it now, you'll get it for breakfast.

NEWSCASTER 2: I can't eat it.

NEWSCASTER 1: Try

NEWSCASTER 2: I can't

NEWSCASTER 1: *(Forcing a bite into* NEWSCASTER 2*'s mouth)* Eat. It won't hurt you.

NEWSCASTER 2: I'll throw up all over your pants.

NEWSCASTER 1: Put it in the refrigerator. *(Transforms back to* COMMERCIAL ANNOUNCER *And sits on desk)*

OTHERS: *(A low chant)* No more food, until you eat your liver.

NEWSCASTER 2: That isn't my liver. That isn't my liver. *(Transforms into* DU PONT REPRESENTATIVE*)* That isn't my liver.

COMMERCIAL ANNOUNCER: When Shell arrived here fifty-eight years ago, Brazil was a simple producer of an awful lot of coffee,…

DANIELLE: …then I'd pack all the items up in my head…

COMMERCIAL ANNOUNCER: …cocoa and rubber.

*(*NEWSCASTERS 4 *and* 5 *enter as Brazilian workers, doing the samba and blowing up prophylactics.)*

DANIELLE: ...and put the pack on my back and hitchhike out to the Penninsula where I could camp out and wade upstream to catch rainbow trout.

COMMERCIAL ANNOUNCER: Today, its industry is growing at a rate of fifteen per cent per year. Its Gross National Product is growing at the exhilarating rate of nine per cent annually.

DANIELLE: Everything I took was dry and compact. I can survive anywhere.

COMMERCIAL ANNOUNCER: Brazil has transformed itself.

DANIELLE: Like during the Berlin wall crisis...or did they call it the Berlin blockade? I don't know, but that was the time when everyone was going to the post office to get plans for how to build your own atomic bomb shelter in your basement.

(DANIELLE *seems bothered that* BARTON *is behaving passively and ignoring her.*)

COMMERCIAL ANNOUNCER: Shell's investments in Brazil have increased just as fast.

DANIELLE: Well, I got the plans and studied them, but I figured all the stuff I'd need for two weeks for me and two others...

COMMERCIAL ANNOUNCER: Shell believes in Brazil.

(WORKER 4 *presents him/her with the blown-up prophylactic.*)

DANIELLE: ...but then I got to thinking of all the waste matter, and how I'd rather be in the outdoors. I think you get a better chance in the out-of-doors.

DU PONT REPRESENTATIVE: DuPont believes in the out-of-doors.

(WORKER 5 *presents her with blown-up prophylactic.*)

DANIELLE: I hate living a lot with my own stink. I know lots of people dig it—it gives them a sense of place. But I decided I'd rather hike up through Canada to the Northwest territories, if it came to holocaust, and wait it out up there in the glaciers.

COMMERCIAL ANNOUNCER: *(Tongue-in-cheek)* But don't believe that you are in Brazil.

(BARTON demonstrates an egg beater.)

(All NEWSCASTERS sit on news desks right and left.)

DANIELLE: If you gotta go, freezing is better than burning.

(During the following song, BARTON uses egg beater on DANIELLE like percussion instrument.)

(All NEWSCASTERS are dressed in pieces of "white tie and tails" for song. Dance transforms from sophisticated cocktail dancing into a dirty mambo, and then they begin to tear each other's clothing off. Flying pieces of clothing, bananas, rubber tires, coffee beans, etc. All NEWSCASTERS sing and dance seductively toward audience:)

NEWSCASTER 2: There is death in Venice, Death in Venice. Anyone can fly down to Rio.

NEWSCASTER 5: This is time for the beguine, bebe, baby,

NEWSCASTER 2: We used to load up our gun and have bebe gun fights, bebe, baby.

NEWSCASTER 5: But now you get hepatitis from the guns, bebe-baby.

ALL NEWSCASTERS: *(Sing and dance sitting on news desks while kicking legs wildly)* 'Cause we's all too dirty to keep clean. Too, too, too dirty to keep clean. We's all Americans under the skin. Ooooohhhh bebe baby, let me in. You got all the way under my skin. Ooooohhhh baby, let's begin. I got to get in. I got to get in. I-I-I wanna get in. I-I-I wanna get in. Come on baby and let me in. *(Faster, wilder dancing)* I got to get in. I got to get in. I-I-I wanna get in. I-I-I wanna get in. We's all Americans under our skin.

(Music fades but continues under dialog.)

*(*BARTON *leaves* DANIELLE.*)*

DANIELLE: A very good friend of mine called me the other day to tell me he was leaving town for good. It gave me the worries.

*(*BARTON *leaps onto chaise with mop head. He and* DANIELLE *look out at audience and turn off rose-pink lamp. A projection of Fred Astaire and Ginger Rogers appears over them.)*

NEWSCASTER: *(At desk in pin spot)* Special from the Brazilian Government to the British Army in Belfast "Keep a stiff upper lip in the thick of the Mick. Signed, Spick."

(Spot fades on NEWSCASTER. *Fred-and-Ginger projection remains. Music builds.)*

(Music stays up strong till blackout.)

(All actors dance off stage.)

END OF PLAY